All rights reserved. International copyright secured.
No part of this book may be reproduced, stored in a retrieval system, or transmitted in any form or by any means—electronic, mechanical, photocopying, recording, or otherwise—without the prior written permission of Learning Engineered Publishing except for inclusion of brief quotations in an acknowledged review.

Title: "Fruit of the Spirit for KIDS"

Written by: Christian A. Dickinson & Morgan Champion-Dickinson

Illustrations by: Learning Engineered LLC
One or more of the illustrations may have been created or altered using an AI tool.

Published by: Learning Engineered Publishing, Tallahassee, Florida
www.LearningEngineeredPublishing.com

Library of Congress Control Number: 2024947754

ISBN (Hardback): 978-1-965741-52-8
First Edition: 2024

Printed & Created in: United States of America

Text and Illustration Copyright © 2024
Learning Engineered Publishing is a division of Learning Engineered LLC and is a subsidiary of Carpe Diem Unlimited Holdings, Inc.

DEDICATION

For Darcy

Galatians 5:22-23

(Amplified Bible)

"But the fruit of the Spirit **[the result of His presence within us]** is love **[unselfish concern for others]**, joy, **[inner]** peace, patience **[not the ability to wait, but how we act while waiting]**, kindness, goodness, faithfulness, gentleness, self-control. Against such things there is no law."

ABOUT THIS BOOK

When our child, Darcy, was born, I realized the importance of teaching the timeless truths of the Bible in a way that would truly resonate with young hearts and minds. The Fruit of the Spirit, as described in Galatians, are profound concepts written to adults, often presented in language that can be challenging for children to grasp.

As parents, educators, and caregivers, we've often found ourselves seeking a bridge to connect these divine teachings with the everyday experiences of kids. That's why we created "Fruit of the Spirit for Kids."

This book isn't just another collection of children's Bible verses; it's a carefully crafted tool designed to:

- **Simplify:** Break down complex spiritual concepts into kid-friendly definitions and actions, making the Fruits of the Spirit easy to understand for young minds.

- **Connect:** Accompany each fruit with a relevant Bible verse, tailored for young readers, to anchor these lessons in Scripture.

- **Inspire:** Pose thought-provoking questions tied to the Fruits of the Spirit to help children reflect on how they can apply these concepts in their daily lives at a developmentally appropriate level. This not only deepens their understanding but also encourages them to take these spiritual lessons and embody them in meaningful actions.

This book is for families, churches, schools, and anyone who wishes to instill these irreplaceable values in the next generation. It's about teaching our children the important things, the permanent things, eternal truths in the Kingdom of the Gospel applied in their everyday lives.

May "Fruit of the Spirit for Kids" be a joyful journey for both you and your child, as together, you explore the love of Jesus through the Fruit of the Spirit, allowing the Holy Spirit's work to manifest in the most beautiful ways.

LOVE

Love is a verb. **Love** is choosing to show kindness and care for others, just as God always loves and cares for us.

1 John 3:18 (ESV)

"Little children, let us not **love** in word or talk but in deed and in truth."

LOVE

God shows us love every day. Can you think
of a kind action you could do today
to show someone love?

JOY

Joy is the deep, lasting gladness in your heart from knowing God, which gives you strength and hope.

Philippians 4:4 (NASB)

"**Rejoice** in the Lord always; again I will say, **rejoice**!"

JOY

Joy is inner gladness. How can you share your joy with others? What gives you joy?

PEACE

Peace is the calm and quiet in your heart that comes from trusting in God, even when things around you are noisy or troubling.

John 14:27 (NASB)

"**Peace** I leave you, My **peace** I give to you; not as the world gives, do I give to you. Do not let your heart be troubled, nor let it be fearful."

PEACE

What is the most peaceful place you have ever been? What did it feel like to be there?

PATIENCE

Patience is waiting calmly and kindly, even when things take a long time, just like God is **patient** with us.

2 Peter 3:9 (NASB)

"The Lord is not slow about His promise, as some count slowness, but is **patient** toward you, not willing for any to perish, but for all to come to repentance."

PATIENCE

Think about a time when you had to wait a very long time. Was it hard to be patient? What helped you be patient while you waited?

KINDNESS

Kindness is showing warmth, care, and generosity toward others, reflecting the **kindness** God shows us.

Ephesians 4:32 (KJV)

"And be ye **kind** one to another, tenderhearted, forgiving one another, even as God for Christ's sake hath forgiven you."

KINDNESS

What is the most kind action someone has done for you? What made it so special?

GOODNESS

Goodness is doing what is right and kind, reflecting God's own **goodness** in everything you do.

Psalm 33:5 (NASB)

"He loves righteousness and justice; The earth is full of the **goodness** of the Lord."

GOODNESS

How can we show God's goodness to those around us? Think of one thing you could do to show goodness to a friend or family member.

FAITHFULNESS

Faithfulness is being loyal, reliable, and true to your commitments, just as God is **faithful** to His promises.

Psalms 89:1 (Amplified Bible)

"I will sing of the goodness and lovingkindness of the Lord forever; with my mouth I will make known Your **faithfulness** from generation to generation."

FAITHFULNESS

Who is someone in your life that you count on? We can always depend on God. How does it feel to have someone you can depend on?

GENTLENESS

Gentleness is being soft in your actions and words, showing care and humility, just as Jesus was **gentle** with others.

Philippians 4:5 (NASB)

"Let your **gentle** spirit be known to all people. The Lord is near."

GENTLENESS

Think about a time when you were gentle. What kind of words and tone of voice did you use to be gentle?

SELF-CONTROL

Self-Control is the ability to manage your desires and actions, choosing what is right over what is easy, just as Jesus showed **self-control** in His life.

Titus 2:12 (ESV)

"Training us to renounce ungodliness and worldly passions, and to live **self-controlled**, upright, and godly lives in the present age."

SELF-CONTROL

Can you think of a time when you felt like getting angry or doing something you knew wasn't right, but you decided to stay calm and make a better choice? How did that show self-control?

www.ingramcontent.com/pod-product-compliance
Lightning Source LLC
Chambersburg PA
CBRC091203010526
44107CB00021B/1233